# Essays on Library and Information Science Education

# Essays on Library and Information Science Education

By

**Bikika Laloo Tariang**
*PhD*

**Ess Ess Publications**
New Delhi

***Essays on Library and Information Science Education***



**ISBN: 978-81-7000-676-3**

**Rs** Rs.400/-
Ess Ess

**First Published 2012**

Published by:
**Ess Ess Publications**
4831/24, Ansari Road,
Darya Ganj,
New Delhi-110 002.
INDIA
Phones: 23260807, 41563444
Fax: 41563334
E-mail: info@essessreference.com
www.essessreference.com

Cover Design by *Patch Creative Unit*

Printed and bound in India at Salasar Imaging Systems.

# Contents

# Preface

The teaching profession is challenging enough but teaching Library and Information Science is all the more challenging. Library and Information Science is not one to fit in comfortably amongst other disciplines being taught in Universities. Its place is amongst vocational or professional courses like Medicine and Engineering. In fact, LIS Education involves a cocktail of competencies (both technical and soft skills) that prepare its products for even non-library professions like Hospitality and Banking (to name a few). Library and Information Science graduates are also amongst the most information literate of the educational harvest as they have been trained to be the "best search engines." All this clearly places LIS Education in a unique position. This book was born out of the author's experience and understanding of that uniqueness.

Discussed here are crucial aspects of LIS Education from teaching methods and tools to teacher qualifications and qualities. The book in no way claims to be complete. The chapters represent the author's personal experiences with, passion for and principles in LIS Education. The author speaks mostly from experience about pedagogy in the following chapters - (*Preparing Students of Librarianship for the Digital Future, Library Science Education in the Digital Era: Some Reliable Teaching*

*Resources for All Times, Teaching Practicum : What Works, The Place of Information and Communication Technology in Library and Information Science Education, Leading by Example: The Faculty's Role in Motivating Information Fluency Skills in Library Science Students*) and competence in faculty (*Own Your Gift, Teaching in the University: Some Personal Experiences, Teaching Versus Research and Publication, Competence in Teachers of Library and Information Science, Leading by Example: The Faculty's Role in Motivating Information Fluency Skills in Library Science Students)*. The much debated issue of the disconnect between LIS Education and actual Library work is discussed in *Librarianship, Theory and Reality : The Chasm.* Underlying all chapters in the book are the two truths that LIS Education is special and that teaching Library and Information Science is a calling.

**Bikika Laloo Tariang**

# The Author

**Bikika Laloo Tariang** (1970-) is a teacher and writer. She completed her schooling from Loreto Convent, Shillong; B.A. in Political Science from St. Mary's College, Shillong; M.L.I.Sc. from North Eastern Hill University (NEHU), Shillong; Ph.D. from Gauhati University, Assam and M.A. in English from Indira Gandhi National Open University.

Starting off as a School Librarian, Bikika went on to teach Library and Information Science and has been carrying out this calling for the last fifteen years (1996-). She is presently Reader in the Department of Library and Information Science (DLIS), North Eastern Hill University (NEHU), Shillong, Meghalaya, India. In her years in the University, Bikika has been involved in the academic and administrative aspects of the profession having taught various papers and held various positions. Included amongst the papers she has taught are *User Studies, Reference Service, Collection Development* and *Research Methodology* while she had also briefly taught *Cataloguing Theory, Fundamentals of Computers* and *Library Management.* Very early in her career, Bikika was placed in charge of the *Library Housekeeping Operations* paper, a task she has been carrying on till date. This Paper involves theoretical aspects of Librarianship being taught in the classroom as well as practical aspects being imparted to the students within the NEHU Central Library. Bikika is also coordinator *Internship Programme* of the DLIS, NEHU, where students of the Department (after completion of their MLISc course) undergo Internship in select college libraries in Shillong city for three months.

Apart from her teaching responsibilities, Bikika has also been actively involved in the profession through her participation in curriculum development, and counseling and placement of students. She has contributed as resource person (within and outside NEHU) and as organizer and co-organizer of various programmes such as conferences, seminars and workshops. She has also presented academic and socially relevant papers at local, national and international meetings.

Her published work includes a book on User Studies titled, *"Information Needs, Information Seeking Behaviour and Users,"* published by Ess Ess Publications, New Delhi; a collection of English short stories titled, *"Dad and the Salesman,"* published by Writers Workshop, Kolkata; a collection of English poems titled, *"Empty Lives,"* and a collection of Khasi poems titled, *"Jingim Ba Suda,"* both printed by Rilum Press, Shillong. Her latest publications are *Shillong Vignettes : Not Your Regular Travel Guide* and *Humour Central*, a collection of her favourite jokes. *Shillong Vignettes*, a collection of vignettes on her hometown has received positive reviews from such iconic magazines as Good Housekeeping and Outlook Traveler. Her articles have appeared in professional journals, Christian magazines and local newspapers.

Bikika is a life member of the *Indian Library Association* (ILA), *Indian Association of Teachers of Library and Information Science* (IATLIS) and *All India Poetess Conference,* and associate life member of the *Poetry*

*Society of India* . She is also a member of the *North Eastern Hill University Teachers' Association* (NEHUTA), the *Meghalaya Tribal Teachers Association* (METTA, the *Weeding Committee- NEHU Central Library,* the *Disciplinary Committee, DLIS, NEHU and the Library Committee, Nongthymmai Presbyterian Church, Shillong.*

# 1

# Own Your Gift

I'm a gifted writer and teacher. Of that I'm sure and have no qualms about saying so. I will not put on false modesty. I'm sick of false modesty and humility. There's enough of that going around. Real humility is not about being coy about our gifts whether physical or intellectual. Or about letting people walk all over us. For a long time I played that game and thought I was the humblest. Now I realize humility goes deeper. The really humble people don't know they're humble. So go ahead, accept that compliment with a "Thank you," and return it where possible. Acknowledge the gifts God has bestowed on you and use them to benefit yourself and the world.

I will not shy away from declaring my gifts when necessary. I reiterate, I'm sure about where I'm gifted. I'm also sure about where I'm *not* gifted. I cannot sing. Period. For a long time I didn't even know what the terms 'alto' and 'soprano' meant. Nor can I paint pretty landscapes or draw *Tintin* type cartoons. Or any type of cartoon for that matter. All of which I wish I could do. Sure I could dabble in these arts and maybe produce things that vaguely resemble landscapes and cartoons. But it's going to take effort. It's not going to come naturally. Because I'm not gifted in these areas. Writing comes naturally to me. So does teaching. These are things I do with ease. That's not to say I'm perfect at either of these. But when God has given me the gift, I start from there and strive on to perfection. Sure I've made mistakes but I've been the better for them.

I started writing for the local newspapers in my final year of school. Simple articles which I now think needed a lot of editing. But I'm proud of those articles all the same. Even before that, some of my essays used to be appreciated by my English teachers. If I remember correctly, one or two of those were even read out to the class.

Lecturing in the University just one year after my post graduation also came naturally despite the fact that until then I had always been this timid, quivering creature. If lecturing is not my gift then explain to me how I am able to stand confidently in front of adult students (some much older than I am) even though I'm petrified of public speaking and group interaction. I used to be tongue tied even at faculty meetings. A former head of my Department had put it simply, "Biki doesn't talk." Whereas when I'm in the classroom, I'm totally transformed. I forget to be nervous. And if truth be told there have been times when I've entered the classroom without my usual quota of preparation. These have been rare of course, but I must say I was able to pull through without major hitches.

However, even amongst teachers, there are categories. After graduating, to earn some pocket money, I officiated at a reputed local boys' school, teaching standard three students for three days. Those were torturous three days from which I took quite a long time to recover. Conclusion – I am not gifted to teach little children. God knew it. The children knew it. And I was pretty surprised when it dawned on me. I fled with a bruised ego. The irony of the matter is that I adore children. And they've always naturally gravitated towards me. My home is always filled with kids. My sister's kids. My neighbours' kids. They come over, play over, eat over and even stay over. We're buddies who call each other up or *sms* each other (they, using their parent's or siblings' cell phones). We remember each other's birthdays. Yes, me and seven and ten year old kids. Yet in the controlled (uncontrollable?) environment of school, we just can't get along. Clearly I'm not gifted to teach young children.

You attend music school only if you're gifted in music. The same goes for painting, interior designing, fashion designing, architecture and whatever else. And yes, even caregiving i.e. the medical and para-medical profession. Sure your five or more years at med school can make a doctor out of you. But then there are doctors and there are doctors if you know what I mean. Haven't we all met relatives or friends who are naturals at caregiving without the 'Dr.' tag attached to their names? And haven't we all met gifted interior designers, architects and musicians who dont have the 'necessary' degrees? So I say go join that fine arts school only if you're sure you're gifted in that area. Go in order to hone your gift.

Sadly the world is full of 'highly qualified' architects, fashion designers, doctors and teachers. They obtain their degrees due to family and peer pressure or due to greed for power and money. They then practice their profession without much impact. The unscrupulous ones, fully aware of their own incompetence, carry on, minting money and sometimes even victimizing their clients. The gifted doctor will throw you out of his chamber if you keep coming to him with imaginary ailments (like my family doctor who told me my problem was my fertile imagination). The ordinary doctor will make money out of your imaginary ailments. The same goes for other professions.

In the area of teaching too, I have personally found how some Ph.D holders can bore their students to death with their pontification. That is why I don't value a Ph.D all that much even though I hold one myself. 'Foreign returned' types with assorted degrees don't impress me until I hear them deliver the goods. Other than the usual promotions and perks, these lofty degrees do nothing for a person or her students. If anything, they only inflate people's egos. You're neither a better human being nor a better teacher on account of your Ph.D. The students especially, gain very little if you're not naturally good at your work. And ultimately aren't they the ones who should benefit from your high degrees? Don't get me wrong, I'm not undermining the importance of a Ph.D or any other high degree. They are necessary for our personal advancement as well as that of our country's education system. If our education system is praiseworthy it is because of the existence of hardworking, qualified and gifted people - our researchers. The keyword here is 'gifted.'

The fact, is God has given everyone a gift or two or three. Everyone. Isn't it amazing how even severely retarded people can be so gifted? We've had physically challenged pianists, singers, painters and many more geniuses. So nobody should say they're not gifted. It's an insult to God. Just find out what your gift is and use it. One way of finding out is to see whether whatever it is comes naturally to you and whether you enjoy it. I know my gifts. They are writing and teaching.

# 2

# Teaching in the University:

## Some Personal Experiences

### INTRODUCTION

Teaching is a learning experience. One believes that any good teacher would agree with that. No amount of training can fully equip a person for all that happens in the classroom. A new entrant to the teaching profession, despite possessing high degrees and (sometimes)-intensive training, is as raw as the students he/she has to face.

Some of my personal 'learning' experiences are discussed below. Probably, these will bring back memories for the veterans in the profession. It is also humbly hoped that the newcomers might learn a few lessons – they are welcome to pick what they might find useful and also to learn not to commit the same mistakes I had.

## PLANNING AND PREPARATION

Over the years, one has discovered that planning and preparation should be intense. Now those in the profession will argue, "that goes without saying". But one *can* tend to take things casually – not spending enough time reading and keeping up to date, depending mostly on textbooks and old class notes. At the University level the students are all adults. Most students will not swallow quietly just anything that the teacher dishes out. It is important to cover all bases. No amount of fine language, humour or friendliness can substitute solid facts and background knowledge about the topic that one is teaching. These (language, humour, friendliness etc.) can only supplement the facts. Ultimately, one's efficiency or the lack of it will show in the assignments, test papers and examination answer scripts that the students submit. A casual approach to planning and preparation will lead to problems like – not being able to properly answer students' questions and even not being able to lecture for a full hour – having not much to say.

## KEEPING UP-TO-DATE

There is no excuse for not keeping up-to-date. Even if one does not have access to such facilities as the INTERNET, most university libraries are well stocked with the latest journals. Admittedly, there are some journals that belong to the 'high – level' category, containing articles on subjects which most of us (particularly in third world countries) are still trying to grasp the meaning of. However most journals contain simple, up-to date articles on topics that one can relate to, and cite in the classroom. Of course, discussion with colleagues is another very important route – especially if these colleagues were one's teachers once. Discussion are meant not only for keeping up-to-date but also for 'learning how to teach'. "Say only things you are confident about" is an advice that I have held onto, since a senior colleague first gave it

For the Library Science teacher, discussion extends to interaction with working Librarians and even getting connected with the field in the form of part time involvement in library services and Library Committees, teaching practicum to one's students, etc.

Having reading as a favourite hobby also helps. My staple diet of newspapers (local, national), newsmagazines and social magazines apart from professional journals, has always stood me in good stead ensuring that I am able to discuss with a fair amount of confidence almost anything under the sun.

Television also has its role of course. For example discussion on the Greenpeace ship 'Rainbow Warrior' that was sunk and buried in New Zealand was possible due to one's daily viewing of the programme 'Lonely Planet' on the Discovery Channel. Teaching is always made livelier when knowledge gained from the mass media is used in the classroom.

## RELATIONSHIP WITH STUDENTS

As mentioned earlier, University students are adults with minds of their own. This is a group that one cannot take for granted, not only because they are adults with minds of their own, but more importantly because without them, one wouldn't be a 'lecturer'. Normally, if one is natural and comfortable with them, half the battle is won. The important thing is not to intimidate them. As a student, one had encountered some Professors (particularly those coming as visiting Fellows) with a variety of degrees (Ph.D., double Ph.D., post doctoral degrees etc.) attached to their names who failed miserably in making the students understand a topic – simply because they only wanted to show how clever they were – always happy to pontificate. Many could not 'come down to our level.' Thus the humble approach, not the 'I know all' approach will make the students interested in the teacher and more importantly – in what he/she has to say.

If we are to earn the respect of the students, the following are some of the points to consider:

(a) Being punctual – it gives a bad impression when one's students are hanging around waiting for the teacher – they will invariably make noise and disturb other teachers' classes. Punctuality also extends to returning of their corrected assignments and test papers as soon as possible.

(b) Partiality is a big no no – their merit should count.

(c) Having a genuine interest in them – they can easily detect phony interest. At the same time there is no need to be over friendly to the extent that they walk all over one. Being friendly is one thing – but when the students' attitude becomes too casual (they start smoking, cracking unhealthy jokes etc. in the presence of the teacher) it cheapens one's position. While one should be approachable, one should not encourage the students to hang around one's room for hours. Sycophancy should not be encouraged. Neither should the students be made totally dependent on the teacher. Some teachers, perhaps out of insecurity, try to go to any lengths to help the students. This results in the students becoming over dependent on the teacher while it gives the teacher a feeling of power. Such a situation produces insecure students who cannot make their own decisions. The teacher is the coach not the player. The teacher also becomes a counselor in some cases.

Students sometimes come with personal problems. All they need is for someone to listen to them. So one should do just that listen. One should not be in a hurry to speak or to condemn them. If one can advise from personal experiences, it would go a long way in gaining the confidence of the students. They then know that one understands. Most importantly, one should be extremely careful not to lose the confidence of the students by gossiping about them and leaking out the confidential information that had been shared. Follow up is also important. One may have to continue to speak with the concerned student over the telephone and even visit them at their homes and hostels. However it must be stressed here again that the students should not become too dependent on the teacher. The teacher should know when to let go. They usually do find their own way ultimately.

(d) A sense of humour helps. Of course the timing of the jokes are important. The students should be made to understand that there is a time for everything. One shouldn't mind taking pot shots at one's self. However the jokes should not be at somebody's expense.

(e) Teachers need to have an exemplary lifestyle. The students *do* notice and discuss what one wears and says or whom one mixes with. A careless word or deed can affect their mindset quite deeply. Bad habits like smoking, drinking, abusive language, etc. should well be avoided or indulged in away from their presence. Controversial personal beliefs or ideas such as religious fanaticism, atheism, political leanings, racial prejudices, sexual preferences etc. would be better kept to oneself or discussed privately.

(f) There are some teachers who have the habit of making the students run errands for them. While this may be necessary in some rare cases, it should not become a habit. Yes, the students sometimes are only too happy to do things for the teacher but one should not take advantage of their respect.

(g) A very serious phenomenon that happens in many universities is a teacher taking credit for a student's work. This is in connection particularly with research work. This is another big no no.

While research requires teamwork between the supervisors and the research scholars, yet there are times when the supervisors misuse their powers and take all the credit while it is the students who do the slogging. There are supervisors who write sundry articles and even receive awards on the basis of their students' work. The students, in good faith, submit their reports to the teachers while the teachers go ahead and publish the information in their own names. This is a sure case of abuse and needs to be nipped in the bud.

## CONCLUSION

One can thus conclude as one had begun – that teaching is a learning experience. Nobody can claim to be a perfect teacher – there will be failures yes- both small and big, but as the old adage assures - 'Failures are stepping stones to success.' So, while training and degrees are necessary – one ultimately learns on the job.

# 3

# Preparing Students of Librarianship for the Digital Future

## INTRODUCTION

While 'digital,' 'digitization' and 'digital library' have become the latest bywords, many of us are still grasping their meaning. This is especially so in some parts of the world where libraries haven't caught up as quickly as in the rest of the world. But things are changing and changing rapidly. Many libraries, particularly University and Special libraries are well on their way to fully entering the digital future. This can be witnessed through the computerization of library activities, the addition of e-resources to the collection, the cooperation through consortia and the actual preparation for full digitization. It is obvious then that traditional practices, though still very relevant, need to be supplemented by the latest trends. This should start at the training level – in Library Schools.

Some Library Schools may be content in walking the well beaten track and refuse to follow latest trends while others may be in such a rush to be seen as 'modern' and 'advanced,' following any and every trend and trampling over the 'outdated' methods that both end up killing the very spirit of Librarianship.

There are about twenty papers being taught in Library Schools through the Master's degree course. These papers range from core (Classification, Cataloguing, User Studies, Reference Service etc.) to optional (Computer Applications, Database Management etc.). A wholesome Library Science curriculum needs to give due emphasis to all papers in order to prepare students for the inevitable digital future.

Library Schools in many countries are now embracing new trends in their curricula without discarding the core and traditional aspects that continue to be relevant. Practical experience in library housekeeping activities is emphasized upon and over the years, intensive computer practical knowledge (in the institution's laboratory) has been added to this in order to equip the students for working in automated libraries. Some of the developments that have been incorporated in Library School syllabi include the following:

a. giving more emphasis to practical/ 'hands-on' aspects (including study tours and computer classes) from the first semester onwards

b. increasing the scope of Information and Communication Technology (ICT) and management courses – with the help of fully functional computer laboratories with computers, printers and Internet connectivity.

c. pruning of obsolete topics

d. emphasizing on the philosophical aspects of LIS so

that graduates come out of the university with a service orientation (this is done through papers on Library Management, Reference Service and the theoretical aspects of Library Housekeeping Operations)

Using teaching methods such as :

e. presentations from students (seminars with power point presentations)

f. knowledge transfer through interaction with working LIS professionals, i.e. Librarians and Library Science faculty from outside who come as Visiting Professors

g. combining the efforts of teachers and librarians in teaching courses (particularly for the practical papers)

h. providing library hours as part of the curriculum

Steps that library schools can further take can include:

1. Having a young and well trained faculty that is up with the times teamed with the 'old horses' who are not afraid to keep up with the trends

2. Admitting quality students. Library Schools should not be dumping grounds for mediocre dropouts from other subjects. This can be ascertained during the admission procedure which should be made stringent, involving strict screening and an entrance test.

3. Monitoring attendance of students strictly where defaulters should be given warnings and even be disallowed from appearing for their examinations if they do not heed warnings

4. Having a cooperative relationship between the Library School and the Library of the parent body, which

allows for more interaction between the students and the Library staff especially where the practical papers are concerned

## PROBLEMS

1. The lack of teaching manpower continues to be a problem in some parts of the world. All faculty members are overburdened with preparation for classes and taking classes, leaving little room for other activities such as research and personal interaction with the students.
2. The practical papers like the Library Housekeeping or internship paper, despite being the corest of the core are sometimes not given their due place in the syllabus being squeezed as they are between other glamorous sounding yet less relevant new papers.
3. Though Library Schools are equipped with computers and Internet facilities, technical glitches such as hanging of computer screens, slow Internet connectivity etc. continue to plague the computers.

## CONCLUSION

There is no denying that the world has already entered the digital future. The information literate is a notch or two above his financially rich but information poor neighbour. It goes without saying therefore that the Library Professional's position is enviable since his 'information loaded education' has prepared him for the digital future.

# 4

# Library Science Education in the Digital Era : Some Reliable Teaching Resources for all Times

## INTRODUCTION

Teaching is teaching, the topic being taught notwithstanding. Every teacher, no matter what discipline he is involved in, will rely and fall back on certain techniques and resources in order to deliver the goods well in the classroom. Over years of experience and through a system of trial and error, knowledge is accumulated, filtered and disseminated by the teacher to the student. There is job satisfaction when one uses his/her God given teaching gift coupled with years of research and preparation. This, in turn, is reflected in the enjoyment, enthusiasm and good grades shown by one's students. This is all the more apparent in the University set –up where the students are adults who are aware of their teachers' capacity and cannot be taken for a ride. Of course a profession is made up of all types of people. There are those who are complacent and see no reason to update their knowledge. They are happy to recycle the knowledge their teachers handed down to them generations ago, without expanding on it themselves. Sadly this is rampant in some third world countries where the system of performance evaluation and tenure are not yet properly carried out as in the West and also where students are pretty docile and will excuse their teachers' shenanigans and incompetence without protests.

The real teachers as mentioned earlier, are those who are gifted for the profession and for whom teaching is a lifelong learning experience. They genuinely love teaching and research and they love their students. And they will go that extra mile in their dedication to the profession. This includes finding and using good information resources to impart to their students.

## LIBRARY AND INFORMATION SCIENCE EDUCATION

Library and Information Science education presents an even more challenging scenario being as it is a cocktail of disciplines. A teacher in this discipline has to be dynamic or be relegated into oblivion. A dedicated Library Science teacher recognizes that he has to read, research and network widely in order to stay relevant. Because "the library is a growing organism," we educators have to keep up with that growth. While the core topics like Classification, Cataloguing and Library Administration/ Management need to be on our fingertips so to speak, we are also having to educate ourselves and our students on a wide range of areas including many aspects of Information Technology, the Internet, new methods of Management and what have you. Every aspect of the curriculum undergoes change rapidly and the Library Science syllabus has to be updated more regularly than those of other disciplines. While entirely new topics such as Information and Communication Technology (ICT) and Library Software Packages have been incorporated into the syllabus, even the core topics like Classification, Cataloguing, Reference Service and Library Management have had to adapt to many new changes. The Library Science teacher is thus in a challenging and dynamic position.

## RELIABLE RESOURCES

Here I describe my experience with the papers I have been teaching in the University over the last fifteen years of service. More specifically, I highlight the information sources that have been my partners and that have served me and my students all through these years.

While my teachers had taught me well and I continue to refer to the notes I took down during my student days, as a teacher I have also put in effort to expand and update my existing knowledge. Over the span of fifteen years and through a system of trial and error, I am now able, to a certain extent, to identify some reliable sources of information that have not failed me so far. Following is a brief description of my experiences with these sources:

### 1. The 'Fundamental Classics'

While quite a few teachers (across disciplines and worldwide) have abandoned print sources altogether and become obsessed with the Internet, depending entirely on it for information (as a result of which they sometimes present incorrect and unreliable information), I am still a firm believer in the 'fundamental classics." These are of course the "old old" books (some may have been digitized) that provide the background of a topic, (any topic in any discipline) – the historical background, the founders, propounders, the definitions, the principles, the components and so on. These are the foundation of the subject and it would be foolish to wish them away or turn our noses up on them. In any case, most of the latest print and web sources still can't help but refer to these old classics.

From personal experience, I have found the following classics very reliable, relevant and useful.

**i. Encyclopedia of Library and Information Science :** This is a source I refer to every year and which I ask my students to refer to also. It is revised from time to time and has authoritative articles written by experts from all over the world. Being a multi-volumed encyclopedia, arranged alphabetically, it is an easy and interesting read

**ii. Librarians' Glossary and Reference Book (Harrod's):** While I do use all kinds of dictionaries, this Glossary is my constant companion. I refer to it almost on a daily basis. This is another classic containing the most authentic definitions, abbreviations and acronyms.

**iii. Annual Review of Information Science and Technology (ARIST) :** As far as reviews go, this is one of the best in the field of Library and Information Science. It is a book I consult regularly, particularly for User Studies, the articles for which usually appear in the first chapter of the Review.

**iv. Books by S.R. Ranganathan :** He is not known as "The Father of Indian Library Science" for nothing, for his works are innovative, solid and foundational and continue to remain relevant to this day. While his language may be a little difficult for many people (especially students) to grasp, yet his are the books that can be trusted for years to come. For my teaching purposes, I have found his Library Manual, Reference Service, Library Book Selection, Library Manual for School, College and Public Libraries and Five Laws of Library Science very authoritative and helpful. The Five Laws especially are like onions and potatoes being applicable as they are in every aspect of the curriculum and the profession. In the papers I have been teaching too I have applied them in one way or the other. For example, to explain how Reference Service fulfils any one of the Laws. The bottom line is that you cannot ignore Ranganathan if you want to teach well.

**v. Books by Denis J. Grogan** : I was first introduced to his work (Science and Technology : An Introduction to the Literature) by my teacher Professor J.C. Binwal in my student days. A book written in simple and interesting language sprinkled with plenty of humour. I continue to consult this book for his interesting description of different information sources. And over the years I have discovered, used and referred my students to many other Grogan classics such as Case Studies in Reference Work and Practical Reference Work.

## 2. Other Classic Authors

Library Science teachers and students will also swear by the following authors:

**William Katz** : How can one talk of Reference Service and not mention William Katz. His white multi-volumd "Introduction To Reference Work," has been and continues to be much loved and used by Library Science teachers and students over the years. Not only does it describe reference work but also individual reference sources in detail.

While *Tom Wilson, Brenda Dervin* and their ilk rule the roost in User Studies, it must be said that their style of writing is not the easiest to grasp. Rather it is *Maurice B.*

*Line* who has made the subject easier to understand and even fun. Like Grogan, he too simplifies the subject and sprinkles his writings with great humour. His report on the humongous INFROSS is so much fun to read precisely for this easy style of writing. For example, in his self deprecating style, he explains the reason for the poor response to the study as being the terror that the respondents felt at the sight of the extremely long questionnaire.

For User Education, books by *Nancy Fjallbrant* and *Ian Malley* can always be relied upon for basic understanding of the topic at hand even though many new books describing newer methods of User Education have emerged.

Most books on Reference Service can also be consulted for User studies as the two topics are intertwined and one cannot be taught without mentioning the other.

Though the Library Housekeeping paper is almost entirely a practical paper where the students are required to work in the Library, yet there are also theoretical aspects of the paper which involve describing the workings of different sections of the Library. For this, books on general Library Administration or Library Management are useful. Besides these, there are also books describing individual library services such as Technical Processing, Circulation, Collection Development etc. which also come in handy.

### 3. New Books

While the classics are indispensible (at least to me), one cannot cope without consulting the latest literature in the field and they are literally exploding into the atmosphere these days. Some exist only as 'noise' to fulfill the 'publish or perish' syndrome that is so prevalent in academia. They are nothing but 'cut and paste' products and could even be counter productive in some cases. However, there are really excellent new books that are coming out in every aspect of our discipline and in the topics that I am teaching, I have found *Tim Owen* (Success at the Enquiry Desk), *Bill Katz,* (Digital Reference Services) and *David Nicholas* (Accessing Information Needs :Tools, Techniques and Concepts for the Internet Age) to be always handy.

## 4. Journals

There is a wide variety of Journals available in the field and I have been personally benefitted from the use of these, both in their print as well as their digitized formats. While a few like *Library Hi-Tech* are specific to their respective topics and those like Library Trends are thematic, there are those that carry articles on a variety of topics in every issue.

For all the papers I am teaching, as well as for my personal research activities, I have found *Journal of Documentation, Aslib Proceedings, JASIS, College and Research Libraries, Journal of Education for Library and Information Science, Journal of Academic Librarianship and Library Administration and Management* to always have something useful.

## 5. Internet Resources

As mentioned earlier, a teacher of Library and Information Science cannot but keep up with changing trends and use of the Internet is thus unavoidable. But I am one of those who are cautious about the Internet and will not lap up everything it throws at me. Research has shown that the first ten hits on Internet Search Engines are not always the best. Sometimes, top slots are bought by unscrupulous types. And while there is a whole array of Search Engines out there, it has become quite laughable to even mention them what with 'google' becoming a verb.

For the academicians, Google Scholar and Google Books are sufficient enough. For emergencies, the 'define:' facility of Google has come in handy for definitions quite a few times. So also the Online Dictionary of Library and Information Science (ODLIS). Project Gutenberg, the Internet Public Library (IPL) and the now defunct Intute are also websites that provide all kinds of reference sources (by subject and language) for quick consultation.

Some researchers swear by the Deep Web with websites like Incy Wincy etc. but I have personally found Google better than these. *Success of course depends on effective searching techniques.*

For User Studies and Reference Service, apart from going through Google for scholarly articles, there are also the personal websites of people like Tom Wilson, Brenda Dervin which contain descriptions of their theories apart from providing tidbits about their personal life.

Many reliable scholarly articles on different environment issues such as Global Warming are available on the Internet for teaching the paper on Environment which most Universities worldwide have made mandatory. Besides, the websites of most Environment Organizations, Institutions and Associations present more authentic and updated information than books. My students and I regularly consult the websites of organizations and institutions such as Greenpeace, PETA, World Wide Fund, UNEP etc.

*Wikipedia?* – Of course anyone who has used the Internet even twice will know that Wikipedia is usually amongst the first ten hits on any search engine. But only a fool would trust this encyclopedia blindly. It is a source that can be edited and updated by anyone and thus is not totally reliable. While it does serve a purpose especially for emergencies, one should rather use it cautiously or avoid it altogether if better sources are available. The better option is to scroll down to the list of references (books, articles, websites) from which the wiki has taken its information and click on those instead. The Wikipedia is at best a means to an end and cannot be used as an end in itself.

## 6. Reading Widely

It helps to be a voracious reader, not only of sources in the field but also of sources in other fields as well. The range of topics can swing from the scholarly to fiction. My interests stretch from the topics that I teach to those that my colleagues teach – particularly Information Technology (because it impacts all aspects of Librarianship including Reference Service and Information Seeking Behaviour), Library Management (which actually covers the theoretical aspects of the Library Housekeeping paper – for example, management of different sections of the library, and aspects on leadership are applicable to the study of the Reference Librarian), Research Methodology (it covers data collection tools like questionnaires, interview and observation which are applicable to User Studies).

Then there is my leisure reading which includes newsmagazine, glossies, non-fiction books (self-help books, biographies and autobiographies), fiction and Christian Literature (books on relationships, peer pressure, leadership, self esteem etc.) which somehow or the other become useful in my classroom lectures. That is not to say that I gossip about celebrities with my students but once in a while, I am somehow able to input information from these sources in the context of my papers. And the success is evident in the lively interactions that the students participate in.

## 7. The Media

Television, newspapers and the radio also have their purposes. Library Science being a dynamic cocktail of disciplines, as mentioned earlier, does lend itself to influences from the media. Information garnered from the local, national and regional news channels, the entertainment channels and especially the lifestyle channels like Discovery Travel and Living, National Geographic, Fox History and Travel and even Animal Planet somehow or the other find mention in my lectures. For example, in describing the activities of Greenpeace, I was able to describe the sinking of its ship, The Rainbow Warrior, based on a programme I had watched on the Discovery Travel and Living channel. And this is just one example of the uses of the media in my classroom lectures. News on environmental issues keep popping up in the media and these are brought to the classroom and discussed with enthusiasm.

## CONCLUSION

There is no winning formula for teaching and no perfect teacher. To each his own. It would be pompous and very foolish of me to conclude that the resources and techniques I am using are enough. On the other hand it is healthy to share one's experiences, particularly with peers. While the above are not the only resources I am using, yet they are the ones I rely on and would like to recommend to other people in the field if they are not already using them.

# 5

# Teaching Practicum : What Works?

## INTRODUCTION

There are a number of papers being taught in Library Schools through the Master's degree course. These papers range from core (Classification, Cataloguing, User Studies, Reference Service) to optional (Computer Applications, Information Sources in various profession). Teaching methods for almost all of these papers involve both theoretical and practical aspects. The division of papers into core and optional (or peripheral) by no means diminishes the importance of the optional papers. A wholesome Library Science curriculum needs to give due emphasis to all papers. Having said that however, it can also not be denied that the part of the curriculum that will come to most use to the future library professional is the one that covers the practical, everyday working of a library involving the activities of the various sections and personnel of the library.

## TITLES OR NAMES FOR THE PAPER

The paper covering practical aspects can either be part of the curriculum or be extra curricular. Coming under different names such as *'field experience'*, *'field work'*, *'practicum'*, *'library housekeeping activities'*, *'internship'* or simply *'job diary'*, this is the 'corest' of the core papers in any Library Science curriculum. Whatever name it comes under, "supervised, on-the-job experience has been considered important," says Stieg (1992). For it is pointless to learn various Classification and Cataloguing schemes, Library Softwares and Indexing Techniques, if one is not taught how to apply them in the actual library scenario. It is this part of the curriculum that will fully equip the freshman for his future role as Library Professional. Thus the teaching of this paper needs careful planning and implementation. This is being done differently by different Library Schools in different parts of the world. For example, in some Library Schools, practical aspects involving library housekeeping activities are taught as part of the curriculum, can be titled any of the names mentioned above and lead to tests and examinations. In other Library Schools, practical aspects are extra curricular with students opting for them voluntarily (especially where no stipend is paid). What works? It is only those who have taught or been taught who will be able to answer the question.

## ADVANTAGES AND DISADVANTAGES

Coleman (1989) has listed the following as advantages and disadvantages of teaching 'practicum':

### Advantages

1. It allows the future librarian the opportunity to practice skills learned in class

2. It heightens the novice's sense of confidence
3. It is an opportunity to make contacts and secure references for future job applications
4. It provides the library school with the opportunity to evaluate the appropriateness of its curriculum relative to the current practice of librarianship
5. It allows the school to maintain its visibility to practitioners

**Disadvantages**

1. The curriculum may already be too crowded
2. Administrative difficulties such as locating and monitoring appropriate practicum sites, might arise
3. Developing and maintaining a successful practicum programme can be a considerable drain on an already tight library school budget, especially when site visits and faculty release time are considered

## SITE OR SITES FOR PRACTICUM

As mentioned earlier, the practical paper is taught differently by different Library Schools. One of the most common practices is where the Library School works closely with the library or libraries (the central library or departmental libraries) within the parent institution or university. The other practice is where the Library School seeks cooperation from all categories (academic, public, special) of libraries outside of the parent institution.

## FACULTY INVOLVEMENT

In Coleman's (1989) study of fifty nine ALA accredited library schools, out of many methods for coordinating practicum, twenty two schools reported that all practicum was coordinated by one faculty member, while twenty schools reported that practicum was coordinated based upon the specialization of the faculty member. The advantages of having a single faculty member coordinating practicum according to Coleman are:

- Assurance of some degree of continuity with the field site supervisors
- Expectation of a fairly consistent level of achievement from the students

The drawback of the above option is that no one faculty member can possess the technical expertise necessary to monitor practicum in all types of libraries. Coleman felt that the option of having the practicum supervised by faculty based upon their expertise alleviates this problem, but this is achieved at the risk of not maintaining continuity with field site supervisors.

## FUNDING

Twenty-five schools in Coleman's ( 1989) study reported that there was no funding to support practicum; twenty three had funding for the requisite faculty travel; three had funding for entertaining the supervising field librarians and two reported paying the supervising field librarians an honorarium.

## MODALITIES

For the practicum paper to be successful and effective, the foundation of the relationship between the Library School and the Library where practical experience is obtained by the students, needs to be unshakeable. The curriculum would ideally include steps like the following:

1. The Library School (in writing) asks the Librarians of

potential partnering libraries for permission to carry out practical classes at the beginning of the session. The Librarians give permission (in writing), also chalking out which sections can be covered on which months according to the convenience of the library staff.

2. According to the Library School's Time-Table, the practical classes are arranged, interspersing them between theory classes, (if practicum is curricular).
3. The teacher in charge of practical classes takes theory classes in the classroom, giving an overview of the working of each section of a library.
4. The students can be divided into groups and be taken to the Libraries to study a section each. The head or in-charge (usually an Assistant Librarian) of the section describes the working of that particular section after which the students are allowed to observe individual activities in different sections and even assist in whichever way they are asked to by the library staff (shelving books, transcribing, filling in forms etc.). All the sections of the Library are covered thus within the session of either two or four semesters. Four semesters would be more ideal. Samples of materials used in every section (such as ordering forms in the Acquisition section, users' registration cards in the Circulation Section, spine labels in the Technical Section and a variety of threads and paper used in the Binding Section) can be distributed to the students for pasting in their reports or Job Diaries.
5. The students note down whatever has been described to them in their notebooks. They are allowed to ask questions to clear their doubts.

6. After the completion of a section, the students submit their 'findings' about that section in loose sheets of paper (stapled together), to the teacher in charge.
7. The teacher in charge evaluates the findings submitted by the students, makes the necessary corrections (including grammar and spellings) and returns the loose sheets to the students.
8. On completion of all the sections of the Library, the students then work on their formal report or Job Diary. This can be an interleaved science laboratory book. Each section of the Library is described under different chapters in the Diary. The samples distributed by the Library are pasted and labeled on the blank side and the text is written on the lined side. The other information should include, a Contents Page, Acknowledgement Page, a Brief Introduction and a Conclusion page.
9. Internal tests and seminars can be conducted after every session.
10. The final reports or Job Diaries are submitted to the teacher in charge a week or so before the commencement of the semester examinations.
11. The Diaries can then be submitted by the teacher in charge to an expert from another University (usually of Professor status) who arrives a day or two before the Viva Voce. He or she evaluates the Diaries and marks them.
12. The Viva Voce is the final step in the process. Here each student is quizzed on his or her experiences during the practicum or internship in the allotted Library.

## PROBLEMS

At the initial stage the teaching of practicum can be a process of trial and error. While some techniques may hit the spot, it has to be admitted that the process can still be bogged down by problems like the following :

1. The number one problem can lie in the inability of the Library School and the Library of the parent body to coordinate their activities to accommodate practicum. Students will not receive the full benefits of this very important part of the curriculum. While theoretical aspects of the paper can be dealt with quite ably by the faculty of the School, they will still fall short of expectations, not being practitioners themselves. Where the practical aspects are concerned, full justice cannot be done to explaining the workings of each section of the Library as the Library staff is already overburdened with its own duties. At best, only a brief overview of each section can be given to the students.

2. The shortage of time is one huge obstacle. Some Library Schools, in order to accommodate newer and more glamorous sounding (but less relevant) papers, end up relegating practicum to the background, squeezing it into one semester or less. To cram such an important paper as practicum into a few months is quite absurd. This paper can be considered the heart of the curriculum. Students need to remember what was taught in practicum long after everything else has been forgotten. But if everything is jammed into their brains so hurriedly and heavily, they would only end up dazed.

Library Schools have taught practicum for years and have devised ways and means for improving it. At least most of them have. (There are those Library Schools that have meted out a step-motherly treatment to this most relevant of papers). For many, it has been a process of trial and error but they have understood its place. It is doubtful whether any one of these Schools has devised a fool proof procedure for teaching this very important paper. Some have succeeded better than others but there's room for improvement for each School. In addition to the steps mentioned earlier, the following can also be taken note of, if practicum is to be effectively taught:

1. The teaching of practicum calls for better coordination between the Library School and participating libraries. Joint meetings need to be held. Written agreements need to be made and binding policies need to be set. If necessary, extra incentives need to be given to the library staff for their role as joint teachers of this paper.

2. The responsibility for this paper should in fact tilt more towards the libraries than to the Library School. The Library School need assign only one teacher to coordinate activities but the rest of the work can be carried out by the libraries. After all, who better to describe routine everyday library activities than those who experience them routinely.

3. Theory classes can be taken by the respective Section Heads of the Libraries in the Seminar Hall of the library. After the theoretical description of a section, the students can immediately be taken to the concerned section for observation of what had been described.

4. Activities related to the actual reports or Job Diaries should also be handled by the Library Staff. The students can submit to them the loose sheets or 'rough copies' for corrections. Only the final copies of Job Diaries need to be submitted to the Library

School (either to the teacher in charge or the Head of the School)

5. Practicum can be expanded to include libraries other than the library of the parent body. The modalities can be worked out in consultation with the staff of those libraries.

6. Internship is another option that can be considered. Here too, the modalities can be sorted out by consulting existing models of Library Schools in other parts of the world that are already conducting internship.

## CONCLUSION

Sproles' and Ratledge's 2004 study had concluded that practical experience throughout the graduate programme – whether through assistantships, internships at local institutions, or part- or full-time employment – should be a part of every student's portfolio. Reeves and Hahn (2010) also wrote along the same lines, in fact going so far as to warn that "without significant library or archives experience (even including in some cases supervisory experience), [LIS] graduates will have a hard time finding themselves qualified for a professional position." This book says Amen to that.

## REFERENCES

Coleman, J.G. (1989) "The Role of Practicum in Library Schools," *Journal of Education for Library and Information Science*, Vol. 30, pp. 19-27

Reeves, R.K. and Hahn, T.B. (2010), "Job Advertisements for Recent Graduates : Advising, Curriculum and Job-seeking Implications," *Journal of Education for Library and Information Science*, Vol. 51, No. 2, p. 117

Sproles, C. and Ratledge, D. (2004), "An Analysis of Entry-level Librarian Ads Published in American Libraries, 1982-2002," *Electronic Journal of Academic and Special Librarianship,* Vol. 5, Nos. 2/3, p.——————-

Stieg, M.F. (1992), "Change and Challenge in Library and Information Science Education," Chicago, American Library Association, p. 120

# 6

# Teaching versus Research and Publication

## INTRODUCTION

A teacher, whatever professional name he or she may be called by, performs one basic function – teaching. Thus what is expected of a school, college or university teacher or instructor is that he or she teach, and teach well. An ideal schoolteacher today, would be a graduate with a professional teaching degree (B.Ed., M.Ed.). A college lecturer is expected to be a postgraduate, preferably a doctorate degree holder, with a B.Ed. or M.Ed. degree and additional teaching qualifications like a National Eligibility Test (NET). Where teachers in universities are concerned, apart from his/her being a postgraduate having a teaching qualification, it is also taken for granted that he/she is either a doctorate degree holder (even a post – doctorate degree holder) or is in the process of acquiring his/her doctorate degree. Added to these qualifications, college and university teachers are expected to continue research and to publish results of research from time to time throughout their careers. Let us now take the case of university teachers specifically. What is required of them has been mentioned above i.e. to teach, to do research (both registered and non-registered) and to publish. The question arises - which is more important – teaching or research and publication? (Research and publication are clubbed together as, what are usually published are results of research – although not all research work may be sent by the researcher for publication.)

## TEACHING

The teachers should ask themselves – "What were we hired for?" "What are we paid for?" "What do the students attend classes for?" In the study, 'Changing Practices in Faculty Evaluation,' Seldin (1991) has made a reference to the importance of teaching, ".....faculty are hired and receive their paychecks for doing one thing, teaching...." It thus goes without saying that teaching is the basic or primary function of all teachers. Many Universities lay stress on the taking of forty or more lectures per semester by each faculty member – added to which are the seminars, tutorials and time spent in guiding the students in their post-graduate and doctoral dissertation work. If the rules are followed to the 'T', the teachers will have fulfilled their primary function to a great extent. They can even expect the products of their university to rank amongst the best in the country.

## RESEARCH AND PUBLICATION

Forty lectures per semester, seminars, tutorials and guidance to students? What ideal teachers that would make them! But what of the quality of their work? Do their qualifications automatically make them good teachers? Are they to give their students, year after year, the same information that they themselves had learnt as students? Surely the bulk of knowledge would have grown over the years since they were themselves students? Surely there is a need to keep up-to-date on the latest developments? After all, this is the 'INTERNET' age. Here is where the need for research becomes important. Research for a university teacher involves working towards a Ph.D. and if he or she so desires, a post- doctorate degree – this is registered research or dissertation research. This kind of research leads to specialization in a specific area giving the teacher expertise in research methods so that he or she might guide other people in their research. It brings prestige to the teacher and makes him or her an asset to the organisation. Apart from this, he or she is expected to continually seek information in order to keep-up-to date in the field and to improve teaching skills or to get his/her work published in a prestigious Journal. This is non-dissertation research without which no teacher can grow.

The first type of research is necessary because a doctorate or post-doctorate degree is expected to be attached to the other qualifications of a university teacher. It is taken for granted that a university teacher *has* a Ph.D. degree or is in the process of acquiring one. Such a degree is of course also important for getting promotions with their corresponding perks – not to speak of the prestige attached to the "Dr." tag. Thus university teachers devote a lot of their time towards attaining this higher degree. Unfortunately, they devote so much of their time towards this end that their basic or primary duty of teaching is neglected – to put it mildly. "Faculty .... are placed in a position where they often neglect their teaching and advising activities in order to attain professional recognition needed for advancement. It is the students who usually suffer the most..." (Seldin, 1991). A study of community on campus by the Carnegie Commission for the

Advancement of Teaching showed that students, especially those at large research universities, often suffer from the faculty members' need to devote most of their time to research and publishing in order to succeed."(Seldin, 1991).

Some teachers are not satisfied with just one Ph.D., they even go for a double Ph.D. But does the 'Dr.' tag attached to one's name automatically make one a better teacher? From experience,(as a student) one found that there were a few teachers with a string of degrees attached to their names who could not 'come down' to the level of the students. They were happy to wax eloquent on a topic for hours just to show how 'clever' they were – boring the students to death in the bargain. Viewed from this angle, working towards a Ph.D. can be said to be a selfish pursuit.

Non-Dissertation research of course is imperative and has its benefits. Some findings of a study conducted in 1998 (Biggs and Bookstein) were that: active researchers are apt to be livelier teachers and more current in their fields; research connects you to the profession; active research and excellent teaching go hand in hand.

A publication is usually a result of research. Biggs and Bookstein (1998) opined that research is important whether or not it results in publication. Results of research are sent for publication in Journals –(the more prestigious the Journal the better), they are read out at conferences and other types of meetings allowing for exposure and visibility of the writer, often even leading to their receiving awards etc.

However the *type* of work being researched and published is also to be analysed. In the study mentioned above, one respondent felt that only "theoretical papers on significant issues' would impress him, another expressed "some skepticism about publication *per se*" but affirmed the value of works with potential for practical application. (Biggs and Bookstein, 1998). There is the danger of a teacher publishing sub-standard work just for the sake of publishing or for the sake of his/her name being seen in print. Who would read or benefit from such work is a question that needs to be considered.

At the other extreme there are those teachers who prefer to 'rest on their laurels.' Having ensconced themselves in this profession, they feel there is nothing more to learn but to consult their ancient notes and face the students – and then at the end of the month take home the fat paycheck. An assistant professor had her desk clear of any reading material. There was *nothing* on it for that matter. "I had read enough when I was doing my Ph.D. – I want to have nothing to do with books or journals now – I just read a little before going to class – most of the time I don't even need to prepare," she said. There are quite a few like her. (This comes from my personal experiences – it is not a generalization.)

Some faculty members don't even dream of consulting a library, any library. They don't seem to feel the need for casual reading of newspapers and newsmagazines – not to speak of even browsing through journals in their field. Research is not a word that can be associated with them. And with Wikipedia on their desktops today, the living is all the more easy. "I have finished my research," they say, referring to the work they had done to acquire their Ph.D. degree.

## TEACHING VERSUS RESEARCH

So which is more important – teaching or research and publication? As has repeatedly been mentioned above, the primary duty of a teacher is to teach and this is to be his/her first priority above all else. The teachers owe it to their students. However their duty does not end in the classroom. They need to interact with the students even outside – in connection with the research being done by the students. So if the teachers themselves do not do research, how can they help the researching students?

However, quite a few faculty members get too engrossed in research projects, attending seminars and conferences and social programmes for 'networking' to the extent that they are hardly seen in the classroom. They forget that it is for the students that they have been appointed and that the students should be their first priority Research and publication should help rather than hinder teaching. "Research wouldn't necessarily improve teaching, but it would tend to strengthen it – to bring currency...,"(Biggs and Bookstein, 1998) For example, in a field like Library and Information Science where knowledge is ever growing, the need for research cannot be over-emphasized. Also, sticking only to the 'traditional' is no longer feasible. The 'in' term is 'interdisciplinarity.' In Biggs' and Bookstein's study, one respondent felt that, "You get better faculty [and] more creative and more useful scholarship if you're interacting with people from other disciplines." Another respondent declared that the sharpest faculty members " participate in the academic world – publishing beyond the journals of the profession."(Biggs and Bookstein 1998).

## CONCLUSION

To conclude therefore, teaching remains the top priority. Research and publication are important – particularly research for keeping up-to-date and teaching better rather than for personal glory. But research and publication should by no means be done at the risk of neglecting the primary duty of teaching.

## REFERENCES

Biggs, M. and Bookstein, A., (1998) "What Constitutes a High Quality M.L.S. Program? Forty Five Faculty Members' Views," *Journal of Education for Library and Information Science,* Vol. 29, No. 1, p35.

Seldin, P.: (1991), "Evaluation of Faculty in LIS Schools," *Journal of Education For Library and Information Science,* Vol.32, Nos. I' , p.212.

# 7

# Leading by Example – the Faculty's Role in Motivating Information Fluency Skills In Library Science Students

## THE DEMAND

How anyone can remain immune to the variety of topics and the ever changing trends in the library profession is quite beyond comprehension. Just when one was getting the hang of traditional information retrieval systems, came the Internet and its search engines. And then there were the burgeoning Social Networking sites. We are having to grasp never heard of before worldwide issues such as genetic engineering, climate change, unspeakable crimes, unimaginable diseases and medical breakthroughs, amazing personalities, appalling political upheavals and so on. And who would people turn to, to decipher these puzzles, than the library professional? Information users the world over, are becoming more aware and thus more demanding. Library Schools are having to keep up with the demand for better information providers (future library professionals) who would help dispel the negative image people have of libraries and their staff. The world needs information providers who would stay many steps ahead of their users. These would thus be people who are fluent in searching for and using information.

## THE SUPPLY

People for Ethical Treatment of Animals (PETA), the late Steve Irwin, Paris Hilton, Julian Assange, Global Warming, thesaurus, cloning, J.K.Rowling. All recognizable topics. Even children would be able to rattle off some of these quite easily. Or so; one would think . And yet, what I have often got in the classroom have been blank stares when any of these topics have come up in the course of my lectures. Lectures given to future librarians, no less. And library users are going to be placed at the mercy of these? Wither school and college education? Their products are entering Library Schools with either blank brains or brains crammed with a mish mash of nonsense. This is especially true in third world countries where education reforms are in their infancy.

Up until they join the University to pursue their degree in Librarianship, many students are clueless about the simplest of issues which may be raging or already passé in the rest of the world outside their own. Yes, information fluency in some parts of the world is quite non-existent. And many youngsters graduate out of academic institutions without having learnt the basic information skills. Some come out with flying colours in their chosen discipline merely by virtue of their phenomenal memory and not by actually understanding the concepts. And they are considered geniuses! Education is text book and examination oriented. And there is not much motivation for holistic learning at home either. Their TV viewing is limited to the soaps and music; radio would usually mean FM, if they tune in at all; and as for reading newspapers or watching the news on TV, that would be asking for too much. The joys of reading are limited to Harry Potter, if at all they read. Using print and electronic reference sources or the media for class assignments is more a last resort than a priority. So, one is compelled to start from 'A' in the Library Science course and hope that one's students would qualify as the information providers they are meant to become. But to what extent would one be able to correct the abysmal ignorance that a majority of the students exhibit within this (usually) two year Masters degree course? Making up for lost years of information literacy is no mean task. And have I mentioned these are future librarians we're training? Yes, those very people who poor ignorant souls are going to turn to expectantly, to guide them through the jungle of information. God save the library user!

As of now, admissions to Library Schools in many parts of the world particularly in third world countries are taken mostly as a last resort by those who have been pushed to it by parents and peers; been denied admissions elsewhere or feel the need to obtain an added degree 'just in case.' They go through the whole course mechanically, some even managing to score top positions by learning things by heart. But what of a love for books, for reading and for readers? How many of these students enrolled in Library Schools are enthralled by the romance and charm of a library, by the smells of old and new books? How excited or delighted are these at looking for and finding information and at arranging and presenting it? A top position or rank in the class will not automatically make one an excellent library professional if one is not already gifted in the area. There are many class toppers who end up as mediocre librarians. The Library Science degree should only draw out one's gift in Librarianship and enhance it. It is not meant to teach people to love libraries and reading, for, if they haven't already had that love before they entered the Library School, they never will (A radical philosophy, with which only a minority will agree). A second class Library Science degree holder with the necessary gifts for and right attitude towards Librarianship, can emerge a better librarian than a topper who learnt things by heart. Of course, the institutions themselves would not easily be able to identify the gifted person at the admissions stage. Sadly, the ' 'would have been best librarian,' may not even gain admission into a Library School merely because his or her poor marks at the graduate level disqualified them, while the 'geniuses' who had never visited libraries in their lifetime, except by compulsion, sail through the entrance tests and interviews. They go on to occupy space, firstly in the Library Schools and then in the libraries where they end up working (on earning their degree with flying colours no doubt, but with no affinity to anything library related).

Wise parents would be good judges of whether their children would be suited for a career in librarianship. The students themselves should be able to identify their gifts and talents by the time they are ready for a Master's degree. Next, the institutions could play their role by devising some methods by which to separate the wheat from the chaff. Perhaps a more intensive and creative screening process would help. Cent per cent results cannot of course be expected, but with the right motivation and methods, the right people would be selected into Library Schools and the world would have true library professionals

- the 'real deal,' instead of mediocrity.

Since changing the education system (till the graduate level) would take some time, (though admittedly, steps in that direction *are* being taken in many countries), the Library Science faculty does what one can during the two years it takes to produce library scientists. And one has to be creative in order to be effective and to save time. The Library Science syllabi in most countries are pretty up-to-date and in step with the digital challenge. However, the danger of textbook learning still lurks around.

## THE SUPPLIERS

Library Science faculties in many parts of the world *have* been keeping up with the trends but they still fall short especially in third world countries where government servants are mollycoddled by their governments. Once one entered the profession, one became a permanent employee. There is no question of tenure and professionalism be damned! However, bodies like the Universities Grants Commissions or Councils are tightening their leashes and making university faculties work for their hefty paychecks and cushy jobs. With the latest UGC regulations emphasizing points for academic performance (publishing, attending seminars, researching etc.) the multitude of university faculty members who had rested on their complacency, have suddenly been stirred up and we now have people collecting points at a frenzied pace. Until recently though, this same mob had been floating smoothly in its state of non-performance, smug in the knowledge that it was a permanent employee of the University and that the non-performance would not impact its advancement in career all that much. And so, the teacher was just as ignorant about trends as the student, since he could recycle his old class notes throughout his career as

University teacher without so much as a whimper from the students or the authorities. So much for information fluency!

## THE STRATEGIES

The Library Science teacher has got to rise above all this. He is training future information providers and must thus be information literate and techno savvy himself. The true university teacher and particularly the true Library Science teacher would first be a learner before imparting knowledge to his students. He is an eternal learner, owing to the dynamism and interdisciplinary of the subject that he is teaching. So he is having to imbibe all kinds of information in order to then impart it to the future librarians/ information providers.

The Library Science teacher needs to lead by example where information fluency is concerned. But complacency being the habit in some parts of the world, most students would follow in the footsteps of their teachers and use the library more as a tourist site. And these are people who will be practically living in libraries in the future! So the casual attitude on the part of faculty will obviously not do. Apart from covering the syllabus as sincerely and effectively as possible, one has also to constantly motivate the class through discussions and anecdotes. Following are initiatives that Library School faculty can initiate to motivate information fluency in their students:

## THE JOYS OF READING

Being a reader helps, for sure. Not all university teachers are readers. Forget scholarly journals, even reading text books and reference books is too much of a chore. And since this laziness is not questioned by the students or the authorities, it suits the teachers just fine to keep recycling the information (notes) their own teachers had given them eons ago. The library is Timbuctoo even if it is located in the same building, and with Wikipedia on the desktop, who needs to venture out of the room? The minority for whom the library and its resources still hold their charm, is the one that is able to direct the students to the right shelf, the right book and the right library staff and is the one that is on the right track.

Promoting reading in students can be attempted through the following 'tricks' (in random order)

i. discussing key authors and their work

ii. suggesting autobiographies and biographies of 'greats' in the profession

iii. lending personal copies of books, journals and articles

iv. keeping students alert by asking questions on current issues found in magazines and newspapers

v. giving library related assignments

vi. extolling the beauty, charm, smell and mystery of libraries and books

## GRASPING TECHNOLOGY

Techno-phobia also needs to be overcome, especially by the faculty. Yes, hard as it may be to believe, faculty in some countries still actually suffer from this disease. There are still those who keep the computers and other paraphernalia the University provides them, as decorative pieces. On the other hand there are those who use these to complete personal tasks (their children's assignments etc.). Then there are the semi-literates who like to appear techno-savvy by sitting before the computer monitor all day and sprinkling technical jargon in every conversation. No, lets grow up and grab the bull by its horns, using technology for the right purposes in order to impart the right kind of information to the students.

Apart from short term courses that are available within Universities and outside, attending seminars and workshops, discussions with colleagues, learning through trial and error and through tutorials provided by websites can be helpful in fighting techno-phobia . One has to make sure of course, that these do not interfere with regular duties.

## WAKING THEM UP TO THEIR CALLING

While it wouldn't matter all that much for students in other disciplines to be inept at information searching and use, it is definitely suicidal for Library Science students to pass out of Library Schools without having understood at least fundamental skills in information gathering and use. The course content in many Library Schools is fairly satisfactory in that area, incorporating both theoretical and practical aspects. However, without the constant reminder of their future role, Library Science students easily revert back to their old habit of memorizing things. One can impress upon the students the magnitude of their role as future librarians through the following persuasions:

i. discussing one's own past experiences as librarian

ii. discussing past pupils of the Department who are making an impact at their workplaces

iii. discussing the repercussions of not satisfying users' information needs

iv. discussing the nobility and worth of the profession

## CONCLUSION

"Librarians are the best search engines," someone

had aptly said. The world should be able to hand over its information problems to librarians. This would be possible only if librarians are adept at finding, packaging and disseminating the right information to the right people. The librarian is expected to be competent. An information literate librarian is a competent librarian. His information literacy starts from his training years at Library School and continues throughout his career. The people from whom he takes his baby steps in information literacy are his teachers at Library School. It goes without saying then that the Library and Information Science teacher needs to be information literate in order to produce "the best search engines."

# 8

# Librarianship, Theory and Reality : The Chasm

## INTRODUCTION

Libraries and library professionals have a major and unique role to play in society. The world is realizing their potential now and it is up to them to prove their worth. This can only happen if the background of the library professionals is secure and foolproof. A proper system of education and a proper running of libraries can ensure this. Unfortunately, this is not always the reality.

Sometimes what one had learnt during one's stint in a Library School is of little or no use once one starts working in a library. This article has resulted from hearing numerous negative comments and complaints aired on meeting professionally trained and newly employed friends. Some time after our batch had completed the Master's degree in Library and Information Science (more than half the group having achieved first class), and after many of us had been absorbed into different libraries, some of the comments that I heard on meeting my old batch mates included, "I've lost touch with classification and cataloguing, in our library we don't classify or catalogue books," "There is a big difference between what I was taught in the Library School and the tasks I have to actually perform at the workplace," "I have to do all the work myself including clerical and maintenance, there is no support staff," "The untrained staff mock me," and so on. These were just the comments of my old classmates, but such comments can also be heard from library professionals who had been in the field for a much longer stint. They however had learnt to adjust to the situation over the years.

According to Oud (2008) "In the process of organizational socialization, new employees face surprises and differences from their pre-existing expectations about the job. Studies have been done to discover what these surprises were so that more effective training and orientation programs can be developed. The findings included several areas of high and low pre-existing knowledge and difference from expectation including job skills and organizational culture. She found that New employees all bring expectations to their new jobs that are based on factors like their previous job experiences, their understandings of the profession, beliefs and experiences held by peers or family, promises made during recruitment, and their evaluation of the work situation during their interview. During initial socialization into their new work situation, the new employee inevitably finds that there are differences from what he or she expected. These differences produce some degree of "reality shock," which is followed by a period of learning how to "fit in" and adjusting to how things work in the new setting.

The use of such studies can improve the ability to prepare future students for work in new digital frontiers and plan continuing education for the Library and Information Science workforce.

Sad but true, the educational preparation for librarianship does not fully equip the newly graduated Library Science students for facing the many challenges of library work. They enter the profession enthusiastically enough, ready to try out all they had learnt in the Library School and endeavouring to become model librarians. Then they come face to face with reality! A reality that is far removed from the cozy environs of Library School; a reality where they have to battle many aspects of the profession which they were never taught about; where many aspects they were taught have to be forgotten about in the absence of proper facilities. They are on their own. They have to improvise and adjust. Some stay on while others lose their enthusiasm and quit.

Apparently this is quite a universal problem i.e. the chasm between Library and Information Science education and librarianship. A survey in 1973 conducted by the Escola De Biblioteconomia in Brazil (De Lemos, 1977) collected testimonies from students and former students of Library Science on the quality of the Library Science education provided by the Universidade Federal De Minas Gerais, Brazil. The survey discovered that there was a need for a more practical approach in the teaching of Library Management. One testimony stressed that the newly graduated librarian was facing difficulties with real life administrative situations. Another survey was conducted by the Departmento de Biblioteconomia of the Universidade de Brasilia, Brazil, among its former students to evaluate the quality of education it was providing. It found, regarding the teaching of Library Management that (a) the course was taught with excessive memorizing of details which hampered a comprehensive understanding of librarianship (b) there was an absence of fundamental principles with merely the learning of routine (c) the course taught did not accompany the latest developments in the field (d) twenty-five per cent of the ex-students surveyed had taken up another University course on completion of their Library studies because they wanted to improve their skills in order to raise the quality of their work.

While the above surveys were done with emphasis on Library Management and may not suffice to portray the whole situation, they can still be extremely useful for the Library Schools to correct deficiencies and avoid overlaps in their course content.

Other studies done over the years have also found a similar chasm between Library Science education and Library work. Elkin and Nankivell (1992) who studied newly qualified Library Science students received fairly discouraging comments such as, "I loathed Library Science School," "The course put me off working in the LIS field," "Dissatisfied with my job at present," "Employers aren't prepared to give me a chance," "Poor support from management ......wrong image of librarianship," "Limited employment openings," etc. Some of the problems their respondents mentioned were poor pay, poor career prospects in LIS, lack of job satisfaction, low morale, too much administration, poor image/status of LIS etc. In 2006, R.S.R Varalakshmi conducted an extensive survey of alumni of the Department of Library and Information Science, Andhra University and employers of Library Science Graduates and found the following:

i. While both alumni and employers are quite satisfied with all aspects of the curriculum, some did feel the need for revision to include such things as an increase in the scope of I.T. and management courses; more practical work from the first semester onwards; the introduction of data warehousing and data mining as full length optional papers; emphasis on e-information sources of the science and corporate sector; and soft and communication skills in the first semester. The alumni were also of the opinion that one of the obsolete topics that needed pruning in the curriculum was the CDS/ISIS software package which should be replaced with more current and relevant packages.

ii. A majority of the alumni vouched for the usefulness of practicum/internship and the study tour which helped them gain adequate practical know-how in order to work in real situations.

iii. The alumni suggested that each paper should have 60 marks for theory and 40 for practicum to be learnt within a library and submitted as a report or assignment. There should also be extended internship and compulsory study tour followed by presentation of experience in a colloquium.

iv. New Library Science graduates are suited for lower and middle strata positions but cannot match the rigorous requirements of important positions.

v. There are varying degrees of professionalism and skills required by various organizations and all aspects need to be taken care of while devising a curriculum

## THE PROBLEM WITH THE SYSTEM OF EDUCATION

Some Library Schools may be content in walking the well beaten track and refuse to follow latest trends while others may be in such a rush to be seen as 'modern' and 'advanced,' following any and every trend and debunking the 'outdated' methods that they end up killing the very spirit of Librarianship.

Moreover, the present master's degree program, which forms the basis for most educational preparation, is constrained in length. With only a few exceptions the M.L.S. program is considered a one-year master's degree, with a curriculum which normally ranges from twenty-seven to forty-five credit hours, or from nine to fifteen courses.

## THE PROBLEM WITH THE LIBRARY SYSTEM

Many libraries, particularly public libraries, are stuck in a rut forever and ever. They rest secure in their age old practices. When criticized about their ineffectiveness, they resort to their favourite complaint of having little or no funds. And so they keep following ancient systems that are alien both to users and to their newly recruited personnel. New recruits enter the profession, enthusiastic with the new ideas they had learnt in Library School only to be confronted with redundant systems. New Library Science graduates particularly in developing countries are in a difficult situation. Not all have the opportunity to put their newly learnt skills to practice. They get employed in various categories of libraries – public libraries, academic libraries, special libraries etc., all of which are run differently from each other. There are some libraries (such as University and special libraries), where facilities are sufficient and in keeping with latest trends, where the staff are constantly on their toes whereas in other libraries (many public libraries), there are limited and outdated facilities and the staff sit mostly idle. Thus while those working in the former category of libraries have their minds well oiled and their skills improving, those in the latter category have rusted skills and very soon lose touch with what they had learnt. No wonder they soon migrate to greener pastures.

**The Solution :** One is not in a position to offer sure shot solutions to the problems mentioned above but researchers (Bramley (1975), Briquet de Lemos(1977), Elkin and Nankivell (1992), Cross (2005), Smith (2006), Varalakshmi (2006) etc.) who have worked in this area have come to a few conclusions a brief summary of which is given below :

1. Restructuring of the curriculum by :
   a. giving more emphasis to practical/ 'hands-on' aspects (including study tour and internship) from the first semester onwards
   b. increasing the scope of I.T. and management courses
   c. pruning of obsolete topics
   d. emphasizing on soft skills such as communication, analytical thinking, decision making, social interaction, positive responsiveness and global perspective
   e. emphasizing on the philosophical aspects of LIS so that graduates come out of the university with a service orientation
   f. offering courses for specialization e.g medical, business, law librarianship etc.
2. Using teaching methods such as :
   a. presentations from students
   b. deputation of students to reputed institutes for practical training
   c. knowledge transfer through interaction with working LIS professionals
   d. making available course ware on the web/online

e. online interaction (virtual classroom)

f. combining the efforts of teachers and librarians in teaching courses

g. providing library hours as part of the curriculum

h. inviting industry leaders to address students

Beyond the expected divergence between what librarians working in different types of institutional settings expect, there also seems to be some inconsistency in the type of educational preparation being demanded. While some writers call for a concentration on the development of overall intellectual abilities in such broad areas as liberal arts, communications skills, and the ability to deal with societal issues and concepts, others stress a general preparation in the fundamentals of the library profession, with the learning of specific skills to follow, largely through on-the-job training. Still others-perhaps primarily the supervisors entrusted with this training-express a preference for individuals already trained to the specific requirements of the job in question, even if necessary at the cost of other more general qualifications.

Other courses which were rated overall as less desirable or totally unimportant include area studies bibliography courses; library history; courses like intellectual freedom, copyright and legal issues, and information theory; and quantitative courses like bibliometrics and in- troduction to research. It must be emphasized that the respondents do not oppose such courses; they merely rate others as more important for the preparation of entry-level professionals.

## CONCLUSION

The time has come for libraries and library professionals particularly in developing countries to rise to the occasion and bridge the gap between theory and reality in the profession.

## REFERENCES

**Bramley, G. (1975), "**World Trends in Library Education," **London, Clive Bingley, p. 186**

**Briquet de Lemos, A.A. (1977), "**Educational Needs for Library Management in a Developing Country. Studies in Library Management," **Vol. 4 , London, Clive Bingley, pp. 13-24**

Cross, J. (2005), "Opportunities for Internships in Library Administration," *Library Administration and Management*, Vol. 19, No. 4, pp. 193-196

Elkin, J. and Nankivell, C. (1992) "Wastage Within the Library and Information Profession : A Report," *Journal of Librarianship and Information Science,* Vol. 24, No. 2, pp. 71-77

Oud, S. (2008), "Adjusting to the Workplace : Transitions Faced by New Academic Librarians," College & Research Libraries, Vol. 69, No. 3, P. 252.

Smith, C.A.(2006), "I Am Not a Specialist : Why We All Need To Be Worrying About Medical Librarianship," *Journal of Education for Library and Information Science*, Vol. 47, No.2, pp. 96-105

Varalakshmi, R.S.R. (2006), "Educating 21st Century LIS Professionals – Needs and Expectations : A Survey of Indian LIS Professionals and Alumni," *Journal of Education for Library and Information Science*, Vol. 47, No.3, pp. 181-199

White H. S. and Paris M. (1985) "Employer Preferences and the Library Education Curriculum," *The Library Quarterly*, Vol. 55, No., pp. 1-33

# 9

# The Place of Information and Communication Technology (ICT) in Library and Information Science Education.

## INTRODUCTION

The classroom at every level of education and worldwide, has undergone drastic transformation over the last decade due to varied developments especially in teaching methods. The developments are such that in some pockets, the very concept of a physical classroom has become alien. We now have 'virtual classrooms,' where the teacher- student connection has been re-defined. If not this, there is at least the use of new technologies such as audiotapes, videotapes and power point presentations that are supplementing traditional methods such as chalk-blackboard and lectures in physical classrooms. In some cases these technologies have replaced the traditional methods of teaching. The main cause of this, as we are well aware is the incorporation of Information and Communication Technology (ICT) into the curriculum of educational institutions.

## INFORMATION AND COMMUNICATION TECHNOLOGIES (ICTS)

Information and communication technology, or ICT, is defined as the combination of informatics technology with other, related technologies, specifically communication technology (UNESCO, 2002). ICTs are now the byword in the functioning of both public and private institutions. Some of them have been around for ages while others emerged over the last half century and continue to develop. ICTs involve media and methods such as the following:

- Hardware facilities like servers, computer terminals or screens, printers, scanners, barcode printers, barcode scanners, Net Servers, CD-ROM Towers, etc.
- Software Facilities like MS Office , Photoshop, Adobe Acrobat Reader, Library management softwares like CDS/ISIS, and digital library softwares like Greenstone, DSpace, etc.
- Telecommunication and networking- Institutional networks or Intranets and the Internet
- Electronic information resources - E-journals, CD-ROM databases, online databases, e-books, web-based resources

The above are only a few of the facilities available through ICT and their role in improving the functioning of all kinds of institutions, be they academic, governmental, medical or business, has been proven over the years. Despite their inevitable shortcomings, the world has become heavily dependant on them and it will not be long before they completely sideline traditional methods of functioning.

## ICT IN EDUCATION

In most parts of the world, what Information and Communication Technology has done is, it has raised the expectations of the teachers and the taught. Its novelty and attractions are quite irresistible to both and in some cases it serves as a status symbol, its weaknesses notwithstanding.

The incorporation of ICT in teaching methods has proved beneficial in terms of clarity, time and money. Pictures *do* speak a thousand words and the multimedia features of ICT have enlivened the classroom atmosphere and in some cases have made classroom teaching bearable (where teachers are dull and incompetent. Competent teachers will use ICT only as a supplementary tool.)

## THE LIBRARY PROFESSION

Library professionals require a 'cocktail of competencies,' from technical ones such as the processing of information sources (classifying, cataloguing etc.), to people skills ("the user is king") to leadership skills (in dealing with administration, finances, personnel, etc). True library professionals are considered the "best search engines" (as someone has wisely said). They are the gatekeepers to information.

Information itself has undergone many births. It is now available in all kinds of formats such as print and electronic. The World Wide Web has spread its tentacles to all areas of life and an individual (especially professionals like scientists and managers) is hard pressed to cope with the information explosion. Hence the need to delegate information search and hence the dependence on Library Professionals. Which is why the Library Professional needs to be adept at handling information in both print and electronic formats.

It is also important to remember that in the Library Trinity (Information Sources + Users + Library Staff), the user is King. It is pointless for a library to have the most qualified staff and the best information sources if the user's information needs are not met. While ICT serves its purpose in providing speedy and precise information, yet the role of the human touch cannot be relegated. People are of all make and types. Most still have 'techno-phobia' and would welcome a helping human hand. They cannot deal with machines or robots. Many are not even sure of what exactly they need, leave alone know how to locate it. The Library Professional thus needs human skills. Like a Doctor, he should gently and tactfully diagnose the information need of the enquirer and then go on to meet that need with the right information sources. Both verbal and non-verbal skills are required in this case. Body language matters. Communication skills and leadership skills make good Library Professionals. While trying to assist one individual, other individuals should not be ignored or kept waiting – thus time management skills are required. The Library Professional needs to understand the psychology of the library user. These are only a few of the qualities a Library Professional should possess over and above his professional qualifications. His is not a mere desk job tied to files and books.

Computerization of Libraries started as far back as 1954 (Kilgour, 1970) with online databases such as Dialog and Datastar being used for information processing and retrieval. Methods for information storage such as microforms (microfilms, microfische), floppy and compact disks have long been used in libraries. The online Science Citation Index meant for information retrieval, in fact was introduced by Eugene Garfield, a Library Professional. Presently, there are softwares for automation of almost all housekeeping operations in libraries. Issues of space and time have also necessitated Digitization (conversion of printed sources into computer readable format). As for the Internet, (which is known to have its roots in Library practices such as information retrieval techniques particularly those propounded by S.R. Ranganathan) its vast and varied reserve of information have made it necessary for the Library Professional to be acquainted with its features in order to filter and present the most relevant information to the demanding and impatient public.

## LIBRARY AND INFORMATION SCIENCE EDUCATION

The above discussion implies that the Library Science Graduate is thus expected to be fully equipped for his future role. While still holding on to traditional skills in information processing and dissemination, he is also expected to grasp all the trends that are fast emerging to make information retrieval and use easier. New hardwares, new softwares , new search engines, new Internet features all have to be on his fingertips if he is to serve the hungry information consumer effectively. And since the obsolescence rate of these technologies is rapid, it is all the more vital that he be able to grasp every new trend as it comes.

Library and Information Science is a vocational course unlike other academic courses. While products of most academic courses wind up in the teaching line, Library Science products are trained mainly for the library profession (which can include being librarian or director of all kinds of libraries) and also for teaching.

Library and Information Science (LIS) Education was probably the first to embrace ICT given that techniques in librarianship also became more advanced over the years and keep changing from year to year.

## TEACHING METHODS FOR LIBRARIANSHIP

With such a future awaiting them, the Library and Information Science pupils are thus expected to be suitably equipped to meet any eventuality. Their education is unique from those of say, the History or Literature graduate. The blackboard and lecture methods continue to be relevant for all aspects of the curriculum. These are then followed by practical, hands-on experience in the form of practicum or internships, usually in libraries.

Processing of library materials or information sources has traditionally been done with the help of printed tools such as the Dewey Decimal Classification Scheme, the Sears List of Subject Headings and the Anglo American Cataloguing Rules. These are slowly but surely being replaced by online techniques such as the Dublin Core and the Library of Congress Subject Headings. Traditional circulation techniques (issuing and receiving of books) are now being replaced with automated systems with the help of library softwares. Information retrieval which used to be done through the card catalogue is now possible through the Online Public Access Catalogue (OPAC) and its web version, the Web OPAC. These are only a few of the operations that have incorporated ICT. It goes without saying then that the Library and Information Science curriculum has had to revamp itself to accommodate all these techniques. The relevant techniques are being taught both theoretically and practically. Major emphasis is laid on

ICT in the Library and Information Science Curriculum with various aspects (hardware and software) of ICT being taught at every semester in the classroom, in computer laboratories and in the institutional libraries themselves.

In first world countries, online education such as the Web-based Information Science Education (WISE) consortium, has been practiced in the last decade. This kind of education involves mostly learning through virtual means.

Writing on competencies required of academic librarians, Bailey (2010) felt, "Most LIS schools offer several courses focused on technological skills and many have a full course devoted to information literacy. These are the courses where aspiring academic librarians should be expected to acquire needed proficiencies."

Since the students are future librarians who will be called upon to search for a variety of information for a variety of people in a variety of formats, they undergo intensive training in this connection during their stint in Library School. They are given assignments on information searching through print and electronic sources. They then present their assignments through Power Point presentations in the classroom. Thus ICT finds place in teaching and learning in LIS education.

Imparting ICT knowledge in Library Schools is being done by qualified teachers who, apart from their MLISc degree also possess diplomas or degrees in all or some major aspects of ICT. Such degrees and diplomas in fact, have become mandatory criteria for new teaching recruits to Library Schools.

## CONCLUSION

ICT is thus more relevant in the Library and

Information Science curriculum than in many other academic courses. The learning of it is not just an academic exercise meant for passing examinations. Library and Information Science graduates are actually expected to be competent in handling ICT if they are to survive in the present automated and digitized library atmosphere.

In view of the above discussion it can be observed that the training received for librarianship is such that if done well, the Library Science Graduate would be competent for even non-library professions such as banking and the hospitality sector, to name a few. It is imperative therefore that the teaching methods in Library and Information Science Education be dynamic and ICT can supplement traditional methods of teaching to good effect.

## REFERENCES

A Curriculum for Schools and Programme of Teacher Development **(2002), Jonathan Anderson (editor), Paris, Unesco, p.13**

Bailey Jr., E.C., (2010), "Educating Future Academic Librarians : An Analysis of Courses in Academic Librarianship," *Journal of Education for Library and Information Science*, Vol. 51, No. 1, p. 41

Barlow, L.J. and Graham, M.E. (1999), The Use of Information and Communication Technologies in Commercial Libraries, *Program*, Vol. 33. No. 2, pp. 116, 117

Kilgour, F. G.(1970), History of Library Computerization, *Journal of Library Automation,* Vol.3, No. 3, pp. 218-229

# 10

# Competence in Teachers of Library and Information Science (LIS)

The ideal faculty member – Rothstein in his 1966 paper, had described the ideal faculty member as follows:

The ideal faculty member in a library school will have several advanced degrees along with practical experience in senior library positions. He will have strong research interests and will have published extensively. He will be broadly versed in all aspects of librarianship and at the same time a specialist in at least one. He will have a personality congenial enough to attract students and yet not so wholesome as to repel colleagues. He will be a mover in the work of library associations. He will be an excellent teacher in the classroom and a wise counselor in the office and committee room. He will be respected and active in the campus community and nationally known in his own discipline. He will be honest, industrious, flexible, profound, cooperative." (Rothstein, 1966)

An ideal such as the above would definitely take the profession many notches up. The existence of such a one of course is humanly impossible. Even Rothstein appreciated that the superhuman he described did not exist.

The Standards for Accreditation, 1972, proposed more believable qualifications and qualities expected of faculty members, that include:

a. a diversity of backgrounds

b. a substantial and pertinent body of library experience

c. advanced degrees from a variety of academic institutions

d. specialized knowledge covering the subjects in the school's curriculum

e. a record of sustained productive scholarship

f. aptitude for educational planning, administration and evaluation

g. close and continuing liaison with the field

"When you locate a person with a first-class mind, an ability to communicate, and a keen sense of vocation, appoint him at all costs, even if his experience is limited – further practical experience can be arranged at a later date and possibly elsewhere." (Dean, 1972)

## TEACHING EFFECTIVENESS

*"The competent teacher, like every other accomplished artist, is born, not made."* (Shera, 1972)

This most apt of statements sums up the whole argument over teachers, no matter which level of education they are involved in. Shera however goes on to qualify the statement (for doubting Thomases) by saying, "Such a generalization [as the above] does not imply that proficient teachers emerge fully robed from some process of spontaneous biological generation. The artist is not born a master of his instrument or his materials. The teacher, too, must grow, and stretch, and learn his art. But without native ability, no amount of pedagogical experience or training will lift the neophyte from mediocrity."

Jencks' and Riesman's (1968), views echo Shera's. They were of the opinion that "most professors become good professors only if it comes easily and naturally. Those who do not have much natural flair seldom know how to begin remedying their failings even if they have the impulse."

As for differentiating between Library School faculty and faculty in other educational institutions, Shera (1972) says, "the qualities that make [faculty] successful in any field are valid for library education."

Teaching was ranked first among 'realizable requisites' for the ideal faculty member by Samuel Rothstein (1966). He was of the opinion that Library Science was technical and therefore required a good teacher to make it palatable and a gifted teacher to make it attractive enough to evoke from the student a response going beyond the call of duty. Blake and Tjoumas (1990) found that there is near unanimity of opinion that faculty teaching effectiveness is a prime component [in faculty evaluation].

Mary Kingsbury's survey of Deans and Directors of sixty-three accredited programmes in 1978 places classroom teaching first in the rank order of existing faculty evaluation criteria.

"Ability to teach," was listed among the essential qualifications for Library Science faculty by The

Association of American Library Schools (AALS) (White, 1961).

"What is it that makes a University important or great?" asked Danton in 1948, and provided the answer himself, "it is above all the presence of men and women who are at once outstanding teachers, productive scholars.....So, too......a Library School."

However, while teaching is important, teaching effectiveness cannot be evaluated or judged externally by members of a discipline or field and, therefore, it cannot and does not earn prestige, feels Wilson (1979).

Methods for assessing teaching effectiveness (Kingsbury, 1978):

a. Peer review

b. Dean or Director review

c. Formal student evaluations

d. Informal review from alumni and/or students

The effectiveness of student evaluations has been stressed upon by Stieg (1992) who feels that although students are often unwilling to be as emphatic on paper as they are in conversation among themselves, such evaluations do identify the most egregious cases of faculty who do not put enough work into the organization of a course and who cannot present material effectively.

A note of caution on such evaluations though, for as Stieg further points out, they (the students) also put a premium on personality. The faculty member who is friendly, kind and always has time to chat is going to come off better than those who do not. [ The danger lies in the faculty member emphasizing these personality traits to cover their incompetence in teaching and research.] According to Stieg, the grades students receive will influence their opinions. [Here again, the integrity of the teacher needs to hold its own and not cower under fear of criticism for giving the students the grades they deserve].

To stress how important teaching is and what percentage of a faculty member's time should be dedicated to it, one can quote Laurent-G Denis' survey of fifty-nine full-time faculty members associated with seven Canadian Library Schools in which "sixty-four per cent of those who responded indicated that ideally teaching should occupy from 40 to 60 percent of their time...."

## PROFESSIONAL/PRACTICAL EXPERIENCE

In the first era of the Library profession's history, faculty members were typically practitioners who had the responsibility of transmitting the best results of front line experience. Sound practical experience, updated as much as possible, plus the personal gifts to teach effectively were the two qualifications expected of those who dedicated their powers to professional learning (White, 1961)

Stieg's (1991) description of faculty of a School of Library and Information Science confirms White's argument. According to her, these faculty members after their Master's, spend a number of years as Librarian, Archivist or Information Specialist before they decide to try Library and Information Science education.

According to Rehman (1994), Library Administrators have been adamant that Library Schools must integrate theory with actual professional practice, which is possible if the instructors are well conversant with real-life problems in a practical setting. Rehman lamented the absence of relevant professional experience and felt that unless faculty members are exposed to real-life problems, they are unable to share professional insights with students. He goes so far as to suggest that future recruitments to Library Schools be restricted only to those who have reasonable experience in the relevant areas and even that such individuals be placed in higher ranks.

In contrast to Rehman's view, is Williamson's (1923) insistence that library experience alone did not qualify one to teach.

Shera (1972) felt "experience can be the source of error as well as of wisdom and [that] practice in a narrow field, however rich it may have been and however long its duration, can make a narrow teacher. ......there is a danger too, in excessive attention to practice, for the kind of library in which a teacher has had experience will almost inevitably color his classroom presentations." He goes on further to suggest that "the teacher's experience should enrich, not dominate, his teaching;" but laments "those who can successfully subordinate their own experience to the larger requirements of instruction are rare." He felt "the anecdote and the personal reminiscence are at one and the same time the enemy and the enrichment of teaching and to master their effective use raises the presentation of the pedagog from histrionics to elucidation."

Over the years, domination of Library School faculty by former practitioners has given way to recruitment of non-practitioners or those with no prior experience of library work. By the later 1930s library educators were abandoning the notion that a battalion of working librarians could comprise an adequate faculty (Biggs,1985).

Having mentioned that, it cannot be denied however that prior experience as librarian sometimes does go a long way in making the teaching experience more comfortable and real both for the teacher and for the taught. "Isolation from the field [can be] the greatest enemy of effective teaching. There is the danger of real pedagogical weakness resulting from faculty remoteness from the field" (Biggs, 1985). Representatives of Dewey's Library School (1887) warned of the great danger of too much theoretical training. John Dean's (1972) views are more balanced. In his opinion, "most library school teachers must construct their courses against a background of reasonably wide experience." According to him, it is well nigh impossible to teach management and operational control unless one has been actively engaged in administration. Assistance to readers cannot adequately be taught by anyone who has never had occasion to help readers and so forth. [Thus] a man going into teaching without appropriate experience will sometimes show a very limited appreciation of practical professional requirements." However, Dean goes on to point out that practical experience in emergent countries unlike in advanced countries, is antiquated and "to appoint those qualified by such experience to the library school teaching staff is only to perpetuate ignorance. Thus, while some professional experience is of value, wherever it is gained, too much of the wrong kind may be disastrous."

## SO WHAT CAN BE THE MIDDLE PATH?

Grotzinger (1966), the biographer of Katherine Sharp describes how Sharp felt that teachers in the Library School should be engaged in some practical work in the Library to prevent them becoming theoretical. According to Biggs (1985), throughout the 1950s and sixties, writers of the library literature continued to urge faculty members to return periodically to the field, in however marginal a capacity.

As faculty in a professional school, Library and Information Science educators need continuing involvement [in the field] for their own enlightenment.

Knowledge of current practice is indispensable, feels Stieg (1992). Dean (1972) also suggests, "it is desirable for teachers to return to the field as practitioners from time to time in order to gain first hand knowledge of current library situations and problems."

## RESEARCH AND PUBLICATION

According to Goldhor (1973), "the person who does research on a continuing basis is a better instructor because of that. Research and teaching are not opposites but are complementary halves of the profound urge to learn the truth and to convey it to others."

While admitting that teaching is important, Wilson (1979) is also of the opinion that teaching cannot be evaluated or judged externally by members of a discipline or field and therefore it cannot and does not earn prestige. In order to attract students, faculty and funding, a preeminent reputation or prestige is craved for by universities. This prestige is generated primarily by writers and researchers..... because it is they who are able to procure what the university needs if it is to remain viable and prosper. While teaching can be recognized internally, researchers and writers alone produce a highly visible product, feels Wilson.

Kathleen M Heim (1984) goes so far as to say that research should be the central activity of university faculty. Hutchins (1956) goes farther than that, insisting that "a university may be a university without doing any teaching. It cannot be one without doing any research."

The emphasis on practical or professional experience in the earlier years of the profession is slowly dying down, making way for more cries for research and publication by faculty members. According to Biggs, (1985) by the 1930s library educators were abandoning the notion that a battalion of working librarians could comprise an adequate faculty. Library educators have been identifying more closely with their colleagues in other disciplines and there are increasingly frequent calls for faculty research and publication. In fact by the 1990s research had obtained such prominence that according to Stieg, it had become "the God of library education."

Biggs and Bookstein (1988) found that the vast majority of Library and Information Science faculty are completely convinced that research is of great importance as it is the principal determinant of a school's reputation. Like faculty in other areas, Library and Information Science faculty also argue that :

- research makes for better teaching
- research keeps the mind alive
- research makes a contribution to knowledge

As with excess in all areas, there is of course danger in overemphasis on or obsession with research. According to a Carnegie Foundation (1990) report, too many universities have sought prestige through research and in the process their mission becomes blurred, standards of research are compromised, and the quality of teaching and learning is disturbingly diminished. Leatherman (1990) supports the above point stressing "overemphasis on publication and research that leads to new knowledge has been good for neither professors nor students, nor, in the end, society itself." According to her, what is needed is an expanded definition of scholarship that includes not only discovery of new knowledge, but the integration of knowledge, the application of knowledge, and teaching.

Research should support teaching else the time spent on it would be meaningless. The fear is that "the object of research has [rarely] any relevance to what students need to know" and that "in many institutions reduction in teaching load accompanies demand for research; some faculty teach little, if at all," (Barzun, 1970; Smith, 1990; Sykes,1988;)

Barzun (1970) exposes the frivolous side of research claiming it "emphasizes the present and the fashionable," and also that it contributes to earlier burnout of University faculty.

Despite the criticisms, research is universally considered as important. Overlooking the self-serving, 'debased,' 'imperfect' and frivolous reasons it is pursued by faculty members, Stieg (1992) says "[research] can be pursued from intellectual curiosity and a love of learning rather than as one more academic exercise, a rite of passage on the way to a life that offers desired social and financial rewards."

She reiterates that there is no doubt that teaching, research and service are expected from every faculty member and concludes that the ideal that every faculty member be a good teacher, professionally active, and produce research, remains.

## NEW COMPETENCIES

The twenty first century is accompanied by a whirlwind of changes in every profession including librarianship. Today's library professional "will not only need the basic core of traditional skills and professional knowledge, but a new list of requirements identified as : flexibility; lifetime learning; people skills; technological skills; business skills including marketing, negotiation, and strategic planning; and valuing diversity," (Library Personnel News 8, 1994). Ojala (1993) also emphasizes new competencies for future librarians entering the cyber world, "the Cybrarian must access electronic and print sources, know navigation skills for all networks, facilitate exchanges with other cybrarians, identify outside experts, and recognize pockets of undiscovered data....Cybrarians organize information so that it is usable. This may include traditional indexing and abstracting but it can also mean adding data to a corporate bulletin board or an enterprise-wide information database. It can mean creating the knowledge base for the networked company, or it can mean interpreting the meaning of the information." In having to educate future digital librarians, LIS schools are having to incorporate digital aspects into their curriculum and the faculty members are having to follow suit in modernizing their teaching methods to include digital librarianship.

Buttlar's and Du Mont's (1996) study of alumni's attitude towards including various competencies in an M.L.S. programme concluded that the five areas that need attention in Library and Information Science Education are:

1. Breadth of curriculum and pedagogical technology to broaden the scope of the interests of Library and Information Science students
2. Greater attention to the external environment (e.g, government relations, societal trends, legal climate, and international developments) that affects the institutions in which students will work.
3. Recognition that libraries are increasingly service-oriented, and that all jobs have service implications
4. Integrating of curricula across functional areas
5. Additional education in interpersonal and communication skills

More recently, Choi's and Rasmussen's (2006) study identified the following skills as important for future digital librarians

## RANKING OF SKILLS AND KNOWLEDGE

| Technology | Library-related | Others |
|---|---|---|
| DL architecture and software | The needs of users | Communication and interpersonal skills |
| Technical and quality standards | Digital archiving and preservation | Project management/ leadership skills |
| Web markup languages | Cataloging | Legal issues |
| Database development and management systems | Metadata Indexing | Grant/proposal writing skills |
| Web design skills | Collection development | Teaching and group presentation skills |

With changes such as the above taking place in librarianship, the LIS teacher is having to keep up in order to impart the right kind of training to the students. There are also new methods like the Web-based Information Science Education (WISE), an online and virtual means of learning, being practiced today (albeit, mostly in advanced countries for now). Thus "there is a need for online faculty to have acceptable knowledge and experience (of content) and ample opportunities to access resources and services, (e.g. technology support, mentoring and educational opportunities) specific to online education," (Montague and Pluzhenskaia, 2007)

## CONCLUSION

The role of the LIS teacher has evolved over

centuries. Changes in libraries meant changes in Library Schools. The LIS teacher has had to adapt to the changing environment and embrace new roles and functions. Information Technology especially, has shaken, if not uprooted, the LIS teacher's position. However, despite all the upheavals, the basics remain - the LIS teacher should first and foremost be a gifted teacher with a love for people, libraries and research. To quote Stieg (1991) again there is no doubt that teaching, research and service are expected from every faculty member and the ideal that every faculty member be a good teacher, professionally active, and produce research, remains.

*"The competent teacher, like every other accomplished artist, is born, not made."* (Shera, 1972)

## REFERENCES

**Barzun, J. (1970),** "The American University: How it Runs, Where it is Going," **New York, Harper, pp. 54-55**

Biggs, M. (1985), "Who/What/Why Should a Library Educator Be?" *Journal of Education for Library and Information Science*, Vol. 25, pp. 262-278.

Biggs, M. and Bookstein, A., (1998) "What Constitutes a High Quality M.L.S. Program? Forty Five Faculty Members' Views, *Journal of Education for Library and Information Science* vol. 29,no. 1, p35.

Blake, V.L.P. and Tjoumas, R. (1990), "Research as a Factor in Faculty Evaluation : The Rules are A-Changin," *Journal of Education for Librarianship*, Vol. 25, p.25

Buttlar, L. & Du Mont, R. (1996), "Library and Information Science Competencies Revisited," *Journal of Education for Library and Information Science*, Vol. 37, No. 1, pp. 44,45, 59

Choi, Y. & Rasmussen, E. (2006), "What is Needed to Educate Future Digital Librarians?" *D-Lib Magazine*, Vol. 12, No. 9, pp. 1, 5, 6, 7

**Danton, J.P. (1949), "The Library Educator," In: Berelson, B. (ed.)** "Education for Librarianship: Papers Presented at the Library Conference, University of Chicago, August 16-21, 1948," **Chicago, American Library Association, pp. 295-296**

**Dean, J. (1972),** "Planning Library Education Programmes : A Study of the Problems Involved in the Management and Operation of Library Schools in the Developing Countries," **London, Andre Deutsch Limited, pp. 58, 59**

**Goldhor, H. (1973), "The Future of Education for Library and Information Service," In:** "Toward the Improvement of Library Education," **Martha Boaz ed., Colorado, Libraries Unlimited, p. 119.**

**Gotzinger, L.A. (1966),** "The Power and the Dignity: Librarianship and Katherine Sharp," New York, Scarecrow Press, p. 83-84

Heim, K. M. (1984), "Dimensions of Faculty Public Service : A Policy Science Approach to Questions of Information Provision," *Journal of Education for Library and Information Science*, Vol. 26, pp. 154-164

"Information Services and Professionals in the Year 2010," **(1994), Library Personnel News 8, pp. 7-8**

**Jencks, C. and Riesman, D. (1968),** "The Academic Revolution," New York, Doubleday, p. 531

Kingsbury, M.E (1982), "How Library Schools Evaluate Faculty Performance," *Journal of Education for Librarianship*, Vol. 22, p. 40

Leatherman, C. (1990), "Definition of Faculty Scholarship Must Be Expanded to Include Teaching, Carnegie Foundation Says," Chronicle of Higher Education, Vol. 37, A1, A16

Montague, R. and Pluzhenskaia, M. (2007), "Web-based Information Science Education (WISE): Collaboration to Explore and Expand Quality in LIS Online Education,"

*Journal of Education for Library and Information Science*, Vol. 48, No. 1, p. 40

Ojala, M. (1993), "Core competencies for Special Library Managers of the Future," *Special Libraries*, 64, pp. 231-234

Rehman, S.U (1994), "Appraisal of Faculty Preparedness by Using Selected Variables," *Journal of Education for Library and Information Science*, Vol. 35, No. 1, p. 29

Rothstein, S. (1966), "The Ideal Faculty Member – Qualifications and Experience," *Journal of Education for Librarianship*, Vol. 7, P. 65

**Shera, J. H. (1972),** "The Foundations of Education for Librarianship," New York, Wiley-Becker and Hayes, Inc., pp. 422, 423, 434, 436, 437

**Smith,P. (1990),** "Killing the Spirit : Higher Education in America," **New York, Viking, p. 7**

**Stieg, M.F. (1992),** "Change and Challenge in Library and Information Science Education," **Chicago, American Library Association, pp. 83, 84, 94,97, 99,100, 105**

**Sykes, C.J. (1988),** "Profscam: Professors and the Demise of Higher Education", **Washington D.C., Regnery Gateway, pp. 58, 59**

**White, C.M. (1961),** "The Origins of the American School," **New York, Scarecrow Press, p.158**

**Williamson, C.C. (1923),** "Training for Library Service : A Report Prepared for the Carnegie Corporation of New York," **Boston, The Merrymount Press, p. 53**

Wilson, P. (1979), "Factors Affecting Research Productivity," *Journal of Education for Librarianship*, Vol. 20, No. 1, p. 8.